THE
BIG
TIME

LeBRON JAMES

AARON FRISCH

CREATIVE  EDUCATION

LeBRON JAMES

TABLE OF CONTENTS

MEET LeBRON

LeBron slowly dribbles the basketball. Suddenly, he cuts toward the basket. He takes two long steps and then leaps. Defenders try to stop him, but LeBron flies too high. Slam dunk!

LeBron James is a star for the Miami Heat. He is one of the best players in the National Basketball Association (NBA). LeBron is so big and fast and *versatile* that he is nicknamed "King James"!

....

LeBron stands 6-foot-8 and weighs 250 pounds

LeBRON'S CHILDHOOD

LeBron was born December 30, 1984, in Akron, Ohio. His mother raised LeBron by herself. LeBron's mom did not make much money, and she changed jobs and apartments a lot.

LeBron's mom Gloria has always been his biggest fan

AKRON, OHIO

GETTING INTO BASKETBALL

LeBron had a hard time getting good grades in school. He was good at sports, though. He especially liked basketball and football. LeBron and some friends soon made up their own basketball team called the "Shooting Stars."

....

LeBron's high school basketball team was called the St. Vincent-St. Mary Fighting Irish

LeBron played basket-ball with the same friends in high school. With LeBron leading the way, his school won three state championships. LeBron was so talented that some of his games were shown on national TV!

LeBron became the most famous high school basketball star ever

THE BIG TIME

After high school, LeBron went into the NBA. He was *drafted* by the Cleveland Cavaliers. As a *rookie*, LeBron scored about 21 points a game. He threw great passes to his teammates and played tough defense, too.

LeBron is known for his highflying slams

LeBron led the Cavaliers to the ***NBA Finals*** in 2007. In 2009 and 2010, he won the NBA Most Valuable Player award. Then LeBron changed teams. He decided to play for the Miami Heat instead.

....

By 2012, LeBron had won the Most Valuable Player award three times

OFF THE COURT

When he is not playing basketball, LeBron likes to spend time with his two sons. He likes to play video games and listen to music, too. LeBron runs a *charity* that helps families who do not have much money.

....

LeBron sometimes visits young fans who are sick

WHAT IS NEXT?

In 2011 and 2012, the Heat got to the NBA Finals. They lost in 2011, but in 2012, LeBron and players like Dwyane Wade helped Miami beat Oklahoma City. LeBron hopes to get his next championship ring soon!

LeBron, Dwyane Wade, and Chris Bosh (right) made the Miami Heat world champions in 2012

WHAT LeBRON SAYS ABOUT ...

HIS GOALS

"I just hope that one day people will think I was one of the best players ever to play in this league."

HIS LOVE OF BASKETBALL

"I don't need too much.... I am just glad I have the game of basketball in my life."

HIS MOM

"My mom and I have always been there for each other. We had some tough times, but she was always there for me."

GLOSSARY

charity a group that works to help other people

drafted picked to be on a team; in a sports draft, teams take turns choosing players

NBA Finals a series of games between the NBA's two best teams to see who the champion will be

rookie a player in his first season

versatile able to do many different things well

READ MORE

Frisch, Aaron. *Miami Heat*. Mankato, Minn.: Creative Education, 2012.

Howell, Brian. *LeBron James: Basketball Icon*. Minneapolis: Abdo, 2011.

WEB SITES

LeBron James
http://www.lebronjames.com/
This is LeBron's own Web site, with information about his life.

Pro Basketball Reference
http://www.basketball-reference.com/players/j/jamesle01.html
This page lists LeBron's statistics and all the honors he has won.

INDEX

PUBLISHED BY Creative Education
P.O. Box 227, Mankato, Minnesota 56002
Creative Education is an imprint of The Creative Company
www.thecreativecompany.us

DESIGN AND PRODUCTION BY Christine Vanderbeek
ART DIRECTION BY Rita Marshall
PRINTED IN the United States of America

PHOTOGRAPHS BY Dreamstime (Dgareri, Ivicans), Getty Images (Issac Baldizon/NBAE, Andrew D. Bernstein/NBAE, Nathaniel S. Butler/NBAE, Al Diaz/Miami Herald/MCT, Ned Dishman/NBAE, Stephen Dunn, Jesse D. Garrabrant/NBAE, Bob Leverone/Sporting News, Greg Nelson/Sports Illustrated, Lucy Nicholson/AFP, Gregory Shamus), iStockphoto (Pingebat)

LIBRARY OF CONGRESS CATALOGING-IN-PUBLICATION DATA
Frisch, Aaron.
LeBron James / Aaron Frisch.
p. cm. — (The big time)
Includes bibliographical references and index.
Summary: An elementary introduction to the life, work, and popularity of LeBron James, a professional basketball star for the Cleveland Cavaliers and Miami Heat who won two Most Valuable Player awards.

ISBN 978-1-60818-337-1
1. James, LeBron—Juvenile literature. 2. Basketball players—United States—Biography—Juvenile literature. 3. African American basketball players—Biography—Juvenile literature. I. Title.
GV884.J3F75 2012
796.332092—dc23 [B]   2012013478

First edition
9 8 7 6 5 4 3 2 1